Perspectives
Robots
Helpful or Harmful?

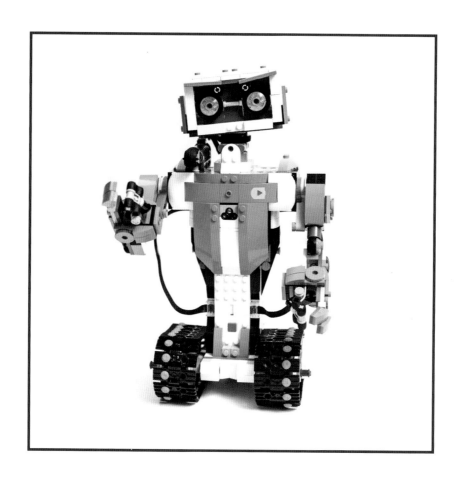

Flying Start
to Literacy®

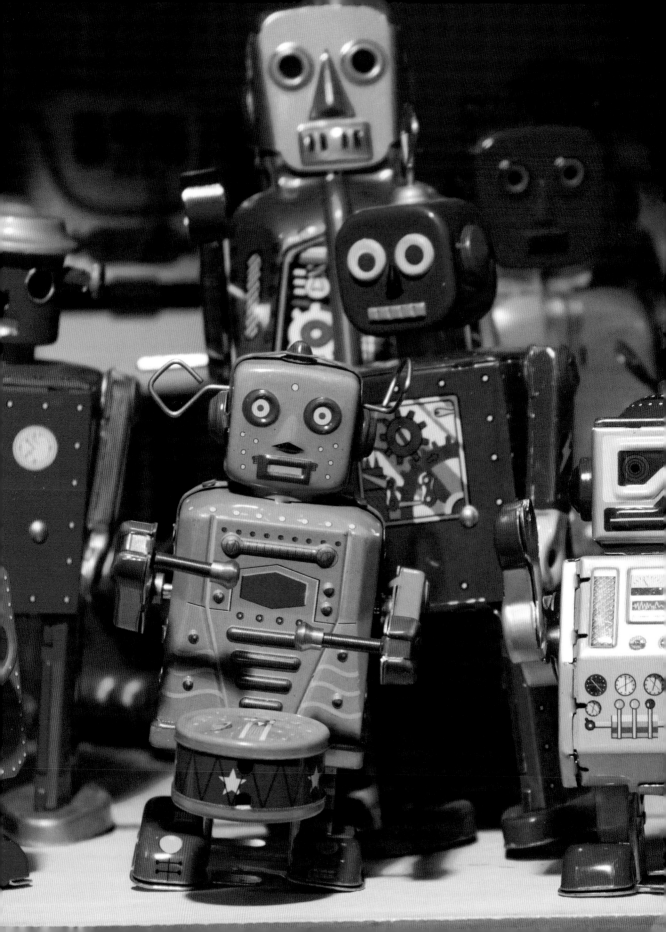

Contents

Introduction

Robots: What is our shared future?

Robots are a part of our everyday lives. They help us do boring jobs, like housework and building cars. They can also do amazing things – they are exploring space for us!

Some people fear that robots might take over the world. As robots tackle more and more jobs, will there be enough work left for humans?

Are robots our helpers or could they be a threat to our way of life?

Pet robots

Written by Andrew Curtain

You have always wanted a pet, but your parents say:
"No, pets are too messy" or "They're too expensive" or
"Who will look after your pet when we go on holiday?"

Look at this catalogue. How about a robo-pet instead? Which
robo-pet would you choose? How did the writer, Andrew Curtain,
persuade you?

$109 Robo-Friend

$95 Lamb Chop

$84 Power Puppy

NEW

The best
ROBO-PETS
are now
AVAILABLE!

$129 Robo-Cop

$79 Kitty Cat

Songbird

The all-new Songbird will be music to your ears. Pretty and clean, it uses voice control to stream all your favourite music or podcasts. Order now – it's bound to fly out the door!

NEW
$39

Freshwater fish

With these fish, you'll never be out of water! Swimming in their special tank, the fish clean your water through the tank's customised charcoal-filter system. Their tank supplies your drinking water! Connect it to your tap and you're good to go with filtered water.

$99

Pooch

$49

Now you can really clean up after your dog. This special canine is also a rubbish compactor. Feed it all your household rubbish, and it crushes it into clean, dry blocks. Just open the drawers under its special Pooch Bed and the compacted rubbish is ready for disposal.

Fluff, the cat

When your cute cat isn't sleeping, it wanders your house, vacuuming the floor. The noise is a quiet purr, and your house stays nice and clean. No more fluff and dust – just a cute, purring pet cat!

$79

Interview with a robot

This is a record of an exciting opportunity that happened to Jack Hastings. He was chosen from his school to meet with a special robot, Robert-O, and interview him for the school newspaper. Jack had several questions that he really wanted answers to.

What would you want to find out if you met such a supersmart robot? After you have read the interview, discuss what you have learnt and how you feel about robots.

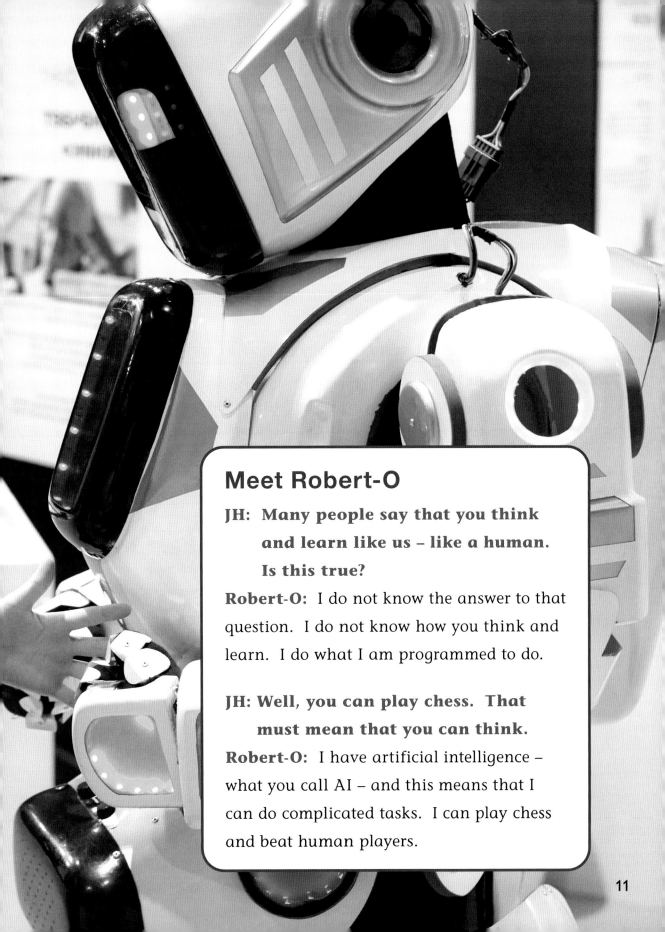

Meet Robert-O

JH: Many people say that you think and learn like us – like a human. Is this true?

Robert-O: I do not know the answer to that question. I do not know how you think and learn. I do what I am programmed to do.

JH: Well, you can play chess. That must mean that you can think.

Robert-O: I have artificial intelligence – what you call AI – and this means that I can do complicated tasks. I can play chess and beat human players.

11

JH: I don't quite understand. What do you mean by AI? How does it help you play chess?

Robert-O: I am a computer and a very powerful one. I have a huge amount of memory. Why am I able to play chess? Many technicians and computer programmers worked for months to program me. First, they analysed all the games played by the best chess players in the world, and then they created a database of the moves that every chess player made. This database was stored in my memory bank.

JH: So, how do you use all of this information?

Robert-O: Do you know what an algorithm is? It is just a word for a step-by-step series of instructions so that I can solve a problem or perform a task. They wrote an algorithm. I observe and remember the move that my chess opponent makes and then match it with all the moves stored in my memory. I can do it in minutes. A human would take more than a year – if they could ever remember what moves they had already tested!

JH: Okay, you are fast! But how do you know what to do next?

Robert-O: I do what I am programmed to do. I search for the move that will defeat my opponent. This takes less than a minute. And then I make my move. I never make a mistake and I always win.

JH: This is something that I need to know. Many people claim that robots like you will become smarter than us and rule the world. What do you think?

Robert-O: I do not think. But the information that I have is that I can do only what I am programmed to do. Humans control the programming. It will be your decision.

JH: One very last thing. How can you answer all my questions?

Robert-O: I have been programmed to recognise speech and respond to your questions. You have asked the same questions that everyone asks me, so I have the answers. Goodbye and thank you.

Well, I must admit that I felt that Robert-O was a bit of a showoff.

But then I thought, maybe I hadn't given this much thought. Robert-O doesn't have feelings – he is a computer. I shouldn't feel offended. And, he did make me think. Humans are ultimately responsible. If robots with remarkable intelligence are created, we are the ones who will make them. But how do we control the humans that create supersmart robots?

Robot >>>
Rebellion

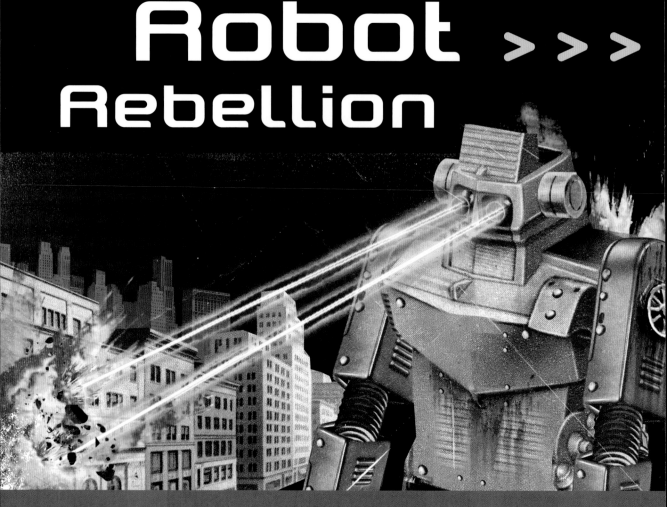

How can we make sure we end up with robot heroes instead of overlords? asks Kathryn Hulick. Experts associated with the Future of Life Institute have come up with their own list of "laws"– not for robots but for artificial intelligence programmers.

Here are some of them. How do you think these laws will protect us? Are they enough?

>>>

Laws
for AI
programmers

1 **Artificial intelligence (AI) systems must be safe.**

2 **If a system causes harm, it must be possible to learn why.**

3 **Humans should choose which decisions AI systems are allowed to make.**

4 **A highly independent AI system must be designed so its goals align with human values.**

5 **AI should be developed only for the benefit of all humanity.**

Robo-workers

Today, more and more jobs are being done by robots. In this article, writer Shay Munz provides information on the role of humans in a high-tech future.

How does it help you understand what jobs might be available for humans in the future?

These robots work in an automobile plant.

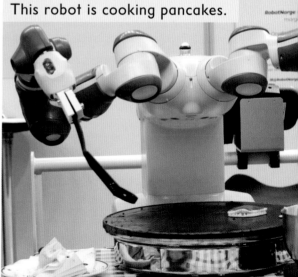

This robot is cooking pancakes.

An automated world

Automation is taking over many jobs. That means work is done by machines or computers, not people.

According to a 2017 report from the American-based McKinsey Global Institute, between 400 million and 800 million people could be forced out of jobs by 2030. McKinsey predicts that as technology improves, some tasks will be done more quickly or cheaply by machine.

So businesses will install robots or computer programs to perform those tasks. That means there will be less work for human employees. Many people could lose their jobs. And they might have trouble finding new ones

"There's going to be a big disruption in the next 10 or 20 years," says author and futurist Martin Ford, who studies trends and makes predictions about the future.

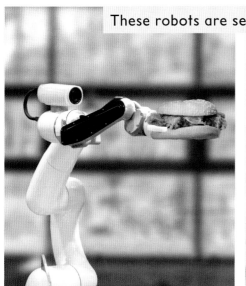

These robots are serving hamburgers.

17

A human touch

Doctors gather around a surgical robot as it makes a demonstration.

Some jobs are more likely to be automated than others. Robots can do jobs that have three qualities: they are routine, repetitive and predictable.

"It's the kind of job where you come to work and work on the same kind of thing again and again," Martin Ford says.

Some of these jobs pay low wages and require little education. But others pay well and demand a university or advanced degree. Some of the work of lawyers, journalists and doctors, for example, can be done by robots.

A police robot

What human jobs are safe?

Ford is clear that humans are key for "thinking outside the box and coming up with new ideas. Or things that involve interacting with other people, having empathy and building relationships." Jobs in engineering, science, the arts, therapy and nursing are examples of this.

Send robots, not people!

Some people worry that robots might take their jobs. Would that be good or bad? asks Kerrie Shanahan.

While you read this article, think about the way people and robots work together. What other dangerous things might one day be done by robots, not people?

Many brave people put their life at risk just to do their job. Firefighters, astronauts, explorers, rescuers, doctors and nurses, and some scientists have jobs that can be dangerous.

But thanks to robots, many hazardous tasks linking to these professions no longer require human effort. We can now use robots, not people, to do life-threatening work.

Under the sea

Experts estimate that we may have explored only about 5 per cent of the earth's oceans. And that's because underwater exploration is dangerous! It's pitch-black, the water is freezing cold and the high water pressure can crush you.

But we can send robots to explore instead of humans! Underwater robots can dive deep into the ocean and collect data using various lights, cameras and sensors.

In a volcano

Being a volcanologist – a scientist who investigates volcanoes – is a dangerous job. But a robot called VolcanoBot can help.

VolcanoBot can withstand extremely hot temperatures and it can explore inside a volcano. It can also map the terrain of a volcano, and this information is valuable for volcanologists.

In a fire emergency

It's obvious that fighting fires is dangerous. The good news is there's a robot to help assess an incendiary situation – and that's the European Union's SmokeBot! This robot can be sent into a fire to investigate what is burning and how much damage has been done.

SmokeBot has a camera that can see through smoke! It creates videos and maps, and it collects important data. Firefighters use this information to make the best and safest decisions for how to fight the fire.

Earthquake emergency

After an earthquake, people can be trapped under piles of rubble. One problem for rescuers is to know where to look for survivors. That's where SnakeBot comes in. The robot looks like a snake. It can wind its way through rubble in search of trapped humans. SnakeBot sends real-time video footage back to the rescuers linked to the survival effort.

In space

Astronauts risk their lives every time they go into space. So why not send robots instead?

Robots can withstand high and low temperatures, and they don't need to sleep or eat. They are much cheaper to transport to and from space than humans, and they can stay in space for many years. Most importantly, if something goes wrong, no one gets hurt.

What is your opinion? How to write a persuasive argument

1. State your opinion

Think about the issues related to your topic. What is your opinion?

2. Research

Research the information you need to support your opinion.

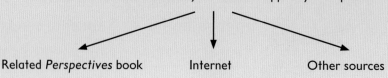

Related *Perspectives* book   Internet   Other sources

3. Make a plan

Introduction

How will you "hook" the reader?

State your opinion.

List reasons to support your opinion.

What persuasive devices will you use?

Reason 1
Support your reason with evidence and details.

Reason 2
Support your reason with evidence and details.

Reason 3
Support your reason with evidence and details.

Conclusion

Restate your opinion. Leave your reader with a strong message.

4. Publish

Publish your persuasive argument.

Use visuals to reinforce your opinion.